Bibliography of
Literature Concerning
Yemenite-Jewish Music

Bibliography of Literature Concerning Yemenite-Jewish Music

by Paul F. Marks

Detroit Studies in
Music Bibliography 27

Information Coordinators, Inc.
Detroit, 1973

Cover design, artwork and photo by Vincent Kibildis, based on a silhouetted tracing of a rock engraving (graffito) showing a row of dancers, accompanied by a drummer, the lead dancer swinging a rope or kerchief. The figures are part of a larger composition on sandstone in the Wadi Kudeirat, Sinai, and dated by E. Anati to the second millenium B. C. E. Courtesy Professor E. Anati, Centre Camuno di Studi Preistorici, Brescia, Italy.

Information Coordinators, Inc.
1435-37 Randolph Street
Detroit, Michigan 48226

CONTENTS

INTRODUCTION

The arrangement of items in this bibliographic survey on Yemenite-Jewish music is according to those works dealing either with music, anthropology, sociology or history which are concerned with the Jewish tradition within the Islamic culture of the Yemen; and by works which deal with more recent developments of the Yemenite-Jewish assimilation into the life of Palestine after 1800 (when a trickle of immigration from the Yemen to Palestine began) and the more intense impact of the wholesale movement of the Yemenite Jewish community of some 50,000 to Israel in 1949-1950.

Studies dealing with the earlier periods of the Yemenite-Jewish tradition have produced much scholarly work in the way of ethnologic studies--though some items are important only for their pioneering efforts in the field. The importance of the Yemenite-Jewish influence on the cultural life of modern Israel has led scholars to see the necessity for a comprehensive study of a still living musical tradition.

During the last fifteen to twenty years, long existing theories have been reappraised as the result of the study of the Yemenite-Jewish musical tradition. The study of polyphonic techniques, for example, among the Yemenite Jews has proven to be important for its application to other cultures formerly thought of as strictly oriented toward monophony and heterophony. In the same vein, theories on the geographic distribution of polyphony have been shown to be at least misguided. [1]

The specific role of women in the society of the Yemenite Jews has produced a good deal of independent research, both ethnographic and musical, on the subject over the past several decades as witnessed in the works of Brauer, Goitein, and Gerson-Kiwi. In the search for more archaic strata of musical expression, ethnomusicologists have been

---

[1] Edith Gerson-Kiwi, "Vocal Folk-Polyphonies of the Western Orient in Jewish Tradition." Yuval. Studies of the Jewish Music Research Center 1:175 1968.

attracted for some time to women's songs in folk societies.[2] This is especially true in studies of Islamic countries, and includes the Jewish women residing in these countries.

Though no single work in this bibliography can be thought of as the definitive work on the Yemenite-Jewish musical tradition, A. Z. Idelsohn (1882-1932) set the finest groundwork for all the research that followed in the fifty years after his monumental Hebräisch-orientalischer Melodienschatz... (Leipzig, 1914-), the first volume of which deals exclusively with Yemenite song. Richard Waterman, in the Bibliography of Asiatic Musics, printed in Notes,[3] clearly stated the situation of Jewish music research prior to Idelsohn:

> ...the music of the ancient Hebrews was for centuries the only Oriental music which seriously engaged the attention of scholars. Even so, most writings on the subject from before the twentieth century, (as well as some later ones), are now of little value save as musico-historical curiosities. Made up chiefly of biblical exegeses, they should be viewed only against the background provided by Sachs, Idelsohn, Lachmann, et. al., utilizing archeology, ethnomusicology and a generally broader scholarship, in addition to the Bible itself; otherwise their many fancied assumptions and hard wrought etymological derivations will remain to hinder the proper understanding of the subject.

The bulk of the works attempting to define the cultural function of the Yemenite-Jewish tradition, through an analysis of musical structure and form, is naturally in the bibliographic section on music literature; however, several of the ethnologic works give fine insights into musical matters, in particular the works of Brauer and Goitein.

I have chosen to include in this bibliography certain fundamental writings on Arabic music as well, as far as that music has influenced Yemenite-Jewish musical style. The writings of H. G. Farmer deal intimately with those aspects of Arabic music which the Yemenite Jew most thoroughly assimilated.

In the area of general Jewish music bibliographies, no work in English has so far surpassed Alfred Sendrey's Bibliography of Jewish

---

[2] Edith Gerson-Kiwi, "Women's Songs from the Yemen: Their Tonal Structures and Forms." The Commonwealth of Music, edited by Gustave Reese and Rose Brandel (in honor of Curt Sachs) (New York, London: The Free Press, Collier-Macmillan, 1965), p. 97.

[3] Richard Waterman, "Bibliography of Asiatic Musics," Notes 5:354 n3 1948.

Music (New York, 1951). Sendrey's work is an enormous study of some 10,000 items that, unfortunately, has not been extended beyond works published in 1944. There is a gap between the publication of Sendrey's Bibliography and the RILM Abstracts (New York, 1967), which is filled adequately neither by the Music Index (Detroit) nor Wolfgang Schmieder's Bibliographie der Musikschriftums (Frankfurt, 1936-1959, edited by Schmieder, however, only from 1950). The Institute of Oriental Studies at the Hebrew University in Jerusalem seems to be taking care that every scholarly work on Jewish music is represented in the RILM Abstracts since the listings for 1967.

Sendrey describes the history of bibliographic writings on Jewish music as one of mostly incomplete, semi-scholarly jumbles, and outlines the development of bibliographic works from the first references to Hebrew music in the Bibliotheca Universalis (Zurich, 1545-1555) by Conrad Gesner (1516-1557) up to his own work.

Among periodicals devoted to Jewish culture, Kyryath Sefer, a bibliographic publication of the Hebrew National and University Library at the Hebrew University, remains an important source of ethnographic and musical studies.

As already implied, the items in this bibliography illustrate the various levels of importance attached to Yemenite-Jewish music across the development of Oriental-Jewish music. Aside from those works dealing specifically with the subject, there are works included in the present bibliography which range from the inclusion of an entire section of Yemenite and Yemenite-Jewish music to those which only mention the subject in passing, and those which either merely include bibliographic references to Yemenite-Jewish music or give distinct explanations of important aspects of the musical-cultural environment in South Arabia.

Jaap Kunst's Ethnomusicology (The Hague, 1959) devotes merely a line of text to the music of the Yemenite Jews, but the work does list nine works on the subject in its own large bibliography. In fact, the bibliography of Kunst's work can be considered the more important part; it surely is the major part. Lachmann's Musik des Orients (Breslau, 1929) is another example of the last type of entry listed above. In each case, items in these categories have been annotated as such.

I would like to thank Dr. Bathja Bayer, of the Jewish Music Research Center at the Hebrew University in Jerusalem, for providing me with access to several items by Yehudah Ratzahby. My wife, Isabel, read the manuscript several times, as proofreader and critic; she deserves more than the usual "thanks" for her encouragement and help.

BIBLIOGRAPHY OF LITERATURE
CONCERNING YEMENITE-JEWISH MUSIC, ANTHROPOLOGY, SOCIOLOGY AND HISTORY

ADLER, Cyrus. "The Shofar, Its Use and Origin." Journal of the American Oriental Society 14:clxxi-clxxv 1890.

ADLER, Israel. "Histoire de la musique religieuse juive." Encyclopédie des musique sacrées, vol. 1, pp. 469-93. Edited and with a preface by Jacques Porte. Paris: Labergerie, 1968. 524p Illustrations.
A description of the evidence and state of research precedes a chronological discussion of religious music from the biblical period to the present. Topics covered include psalmody, biblical cantillation (accent signs and cheironomy), the earliest musical evidence (ms. of Obadiah the Norman proselyte, ca. 1102-1150), the development of hymnody and cantillation in the Middle Ages, art music in Europe (17th and 18th centuries), the traditions of the Sepharidic community and others outside of Europe, the cantoral art in central Europe, the reform movement, and the first systematic collections.

_____. "Juive (Musique)." Encyclopédie de la Musique, vol. 2, pp. 640-54. Paris: Fasquelle, 1959.
Several quotations of group performances of Ḥazzanut in Oriental Jewish communities are related by the Jewish convert Samawál ibn Yaha' al-Magrabi, and others.

APEL, Willi. "Jewish Music." Harvard Dictionary of Music. 1944, pp. 379-83. 2nd ed, pp. 444-47. Cambridge, Mass.: Harvard University Press, 1969.

AVENARY, Hanoch [formerly Enoch Herbert Loewenstein]. "Abu Salt's Treatise on Music." Musica Disciplina 6:27-32 1952. Fasc. 1-3.

_____. "Formal Structure of Psalms and Canticles in Early Jewish and Christian Chant." Musica Disciplina 7:1-13 1953.
Discussion of historical documentation and forms of ancient Hebrew antiphony.

AVENARY, Hanoch. "Geschichte der jüdischen Musik: Literatur." Musik in Geschichte und Gegenwart, vol. 7. Edited by Friedrich Blume. Kassel, Basel: Bärenreiter, 1958. Cols. 258-61.

_____. Magic, Symbolism, and Allegory of the Old Hebrew Sound Instruments, vol. 2, pp. 1-33. Florence: Collectanea Historiae Musicae, 1956.

_____. "The Roots of Synagogal Song in the Near Eastern Communities (Music)." Encyclopaedia Judaica, vol. 12. Edited by Cecil Roth and Geoffrey Wigodor. Jerusalem: Keter Publishing House; New York: Macmillan, 1971-1972. Cols. 554-678. [Yemenite responsorial psalmody, cols. 575-6.]

BACHER, Wilhelm. "Ein hebräische-arabische Liederbuch aus Jemen." Festschrift für Allgemeine Anthropologie, pp. 10-32. Berlin, 1903.

BAYER, Bathja. "H. N. Bialik ve-han-neginah ha-mizraḥit" [H. N. Bialik and Oriental Melody]. Tatzlil 7:149 1967. In Hebrew with English resumé.
Concerning Bialik's "approbation of an Oriental-Jewish Diwân, 'Šîrê yisra-el be-eres haqqedem'" (Istanbul, 1921). Bialik calls for new ethnological techniques for the collection of Oriental folk song. He forsees the renewal of Jewish song in Oriental melody.

_____. "Gradation of Folk and Art Elements in Traditional Jewish Musical Culture (Music)." Encyclopaedia Judaica, vol. 12. Edited by Cecil Roth and Geoffrey Wigodor. Jerusalem: Keter Publishing House; New York: Macmillan, 1971-1972. Cols. 667-8.

_____. The Material Relics of Music in Ancient Palestine and Its Environs. London: Universal Edition, 1964. 178p
Reviewed in Musical Opinion 87:374 n1038 March 1964.

BERL, Heinrich. Der Judentum in der Musik. Stuttgart, Berlin, Leipzig: Deutsche Verlags Anstalt, 1926. 241p
Contains a discussion of Oriental elements in Jewish music.

BIBLIOGRAPHIE DES MUSIKSCHRIFTUMS. Herausgegeben im Auftrage des Instituts für deutsche Musikforschung. Stiftung der preussischer Kulturbesitz. Frankfurt am Main: F. Hofmeister, 1936-1959 (semi-annual, 1936; annual, 1937-1949; biennial, Wolfgang Schmieder, ed., 1950-1959); for 1960, Hofheim am Taunus: F. Hofmeister, 1968. 181p

BINDER, Abraham Wolf. "Jewish Music." Encyclopedia of the Arts, pp. 520-27. Edited by D. G. Runes and H. G. Schrickel. New York: Philosophical Library, 1946.

BORREL, Eugène. "La Musique Orientale." Cahiers du Sud 22:98-100
    n175 1935.

BROWN, Noah. "The Music of the Orient." Hallel (Jerusalem) 1:3-54
    1930. In Hebrew.

BROD, Max. "Judische Volksmelodien." Der Jude (Berlin) 1:344 n1
    1916-1917.

COHN, Francis Lyon. "Folk Music Survival in Jewish Worship Music."
    Journal of the Folk Song Society (London) 1:1-9 1899.

    _____. "Music." Jewish Encyclopedia, vol. 9, pp. 110-35. Edited by
    S. Singer. New York: KTAV Publishing House, 1964.

COLLAER, Paul. "Arabe (Musique)." Encyclopédie de la Musique,
    vol. 1, pp. 284-89. Paris: Fasquelle, 1959.

COMBARIEN, J. La. La Musique et la Magie. Paris, 1909.

CROSSLEY-HOLLAND, Peter. International Catalogue of Records of
    the Folk and Classical Music of the Orient.
    Reviewed in Recorded Sound n10:100-101 April 1963.

    _____. "Non-Western Music: The Jews." The Pelican History of Music,
    vol. 1, pp. 104-117. Edited by Alec Robertson and Denis Stevens.
    Baltimore: Penguin Books, 1960.

DALAKOVA, Katya and Fred Beck. Dances of Palestine. New York:
    B'nai Brith Hillel Foundation, 1947. 32p

DALMAN, Gustav Hermann. "Palästinische Lieder." Oriental Studies,
    pp. 37-89. Baltimore: John Hopkins Press, 1926.

DANIEL, Francisco Salvador. The Music and Musical Instruments of the
    Arab; with an Introduction on How to Appreciate Arab Music.
    Edited with notes, memoirs, bibliography, and 30 examples by H.
    G. Farmer. London: W. Reeves, 1915. xii + 272p

ECKER, Lawrence. Arabischer, provenzalischer, und deutscher
    Minnesang; eine motivegeschichtliche Untersuchung. Bern,
    Leipzig, 1932.
    With references to western Asiatic Hebrew music.

EISENSTEIN, Judah David. Encyclopedia of All Matters Concerning
    Jews and Judaism, 10 vols. "Zmirot," vol. 4, pp. 234-5; "Te'
    anim," vol. 5, pp. 27-9; "Perek Shira," vol. 10, pp. 113-14. New
    York, 1907. In Hebrew.

ENGEL, Carl. The Music of the Most Ancient Nations. London: J. Murray, 1864; W. Reeves, 1911, 1920. 380p

_____. Musical Myths and Facts. London: W. Reeves, 1876. 276p

D'ERLANGER, Baron Rodolphe. Melodies Tunisiennes, Hispano-Arabes, Arabo-Berberes, Juive, Negre. Edited and transcribed by Baron d'Erlanger. Paris: P. Guenther, 1937. 16p

ERNST, David. La Musique Chez Les Juifs. Paris, 1873.

EWEN, David. Hebrew Music. New York: Bloch, 1931. 65p
A general review for the layman.

FARMER, Henry George. The Arabian Influences on Musical Theory. London: W. Reeves, 1925. 22p See also "Clues for the Arabian Influences on Musical Theory." Journal of the Royal Asiatic Society, part 1, 1925.

_____. Historical Facts for the Arabian Musical Influence. "Hebrews," pp. 19, 22, 26, 31, 60, 68, 156-8, 173, 178-9, 296. London: W. Reeves, 1930. 376p

_____. A History of Arabian Music to the Thirteenth Century. London: Luzac, 1929. xv + 265p References to Hebrew music, pp. 2-4, 7, 17, 22; references to Judeo-Arabic musicians, pp. 212, 221.

_____. The Minstrelsy of the Arabian Nights: A Study of Music and Musicians in the Arabic "Alf Lâila wa Lâila." Deardsen: Scot, 1945. 53p

_____. The Sources of Arabian Music; an Annotated Bibliography of Arabic Manuscripts Which Deal with the Theory, Practise and History of Arabian Music from the Eighth to the Seventeenth Century. Leyden: E. J. Brill, 1965. xxvi + 71p

FINESINGER, Sol Baruch. "Musical Instruments in the Old Testament." Hebrew Union College Annual (Cincinnati) 3:73-5 1926.

FORKEL, Johann Nicolaus. "Schriften zur Geschichte der Musik bey den Hebräern." Allgemeine Literatur der Musik, pp. 33-44. Compiled and edited by J. N. Forkel. Leipzig: Breitkopf and Härtel, 1792. Reprint. Hildesheim: Georg Olms, 1962. 540p

FRANKEL, Ludwig August. The Jews in the East 1:183-4, 275-6, 279-80; 2:84-5 (References to the manners and customs of the Jews in the Orient). Translated from the German by P. Beaton. London: Hurst and Blackett, 1859.
Contains information about the musical performance of the Jews in western Asia. The work is abridged translation from the German of Frankel's Nach Jerusalem.

FREEDMAN, A. S. "The Folksinger: A Note on Ethnocentrism." Ethnomusicology 9:154-6 n2 1965.

FRIEDLANDER, Arthur M. Facts and Figures Relating to Hebrew Music. London: Reeves, 1924. 73p

FRIEDMANN, Aron. Der Synagogale Gesang. Berlin: C. Boas, 1904. 99p

GERSON-KIWI, Edith. "Folk Song: Jewish." Grove's Dictionary of Music and Musicians, vol. 3, 5th edition, pp. 304-313. Edited by Eric Blom. London: Macmillan, 1954.

_____. "Jerusalem Archive for Oriental Music. Wege und Zeile des jerusalemer Archivs für orientalische Musik." Musica Hebraica 1: 40-42 1938.

_____. "Jüdische Volksmusik." Die Musik in Geschichte und Gegenwart, vol. 7. Edited by Friedrich Blume. Kassel, Basel: Bärenreiter, 1958. Cols. 261-80.

_____. "Migrations and Mutations of Oriental Folk Instruments." Journal of the International Folk Music Council 4:16-19 1952.

_____. The Music of the Orient--Ancient and Modern. Tel Aviv: Israel Music Institute, 1949. In Hebrew.

_____. "The Musicians of the Orient." Edoth. Organ of the Israel Society for Folklore and Ethnology 1:227-33 1941.

_____. "Musicology in Israel." Acta Musicologica 30:17-20 n1-2 1958.

_____. "Musique dans la Bible." Dictionnaire de la Bible, vol. 5, suppl. Edited by A. Pirot. Paris, 1957. Cols. 1411-68.

_____. "Religious Chant--A Pan-Asiatic Conception of Music." Journal of the International Folk Music Council 13:64-7 1961.

GERSON-KIWI, Edith. "Synthesis and Symbiosis of Melodic Styles in
Israel." Bath-Kol (Tel Aviv) 1:15-18 1955. In Hebrew.
Originally read as a paper at the Congresso di Musica Mediterranea,
Palermo, Sicily, 1954.

_____. "Šittôt has-selîl šel ham-mizrach; hithawwût we hitpattehût"
[Tone-Systems of the Orient; Genesis and Development]. Tatzlil 8:
23-6 1968. In Hebrew with an English summary.

_____. "Towards an Exact Transcription of Tone Relations." Acta
Musicologica 25:80-83 n1-3 1953.

_____. "The Transcription of Oriental Music." Communities 3:181-3
1947-1948; Edoth 3:17-19 1947-1948; Journal of the International
Folk Music Council 1:68-70 1949.

_____. "Vocal Folk-Polyphonies of the Western Orient in Jewish
Tradition." Yuval; Studies of the Jewish Music Research Center,
vol. 1, pp. 169-93. Edited by Israel Adler, Hanoch Avenary,
Bathja Bayer. Jerusalem: Hebrew University Press, 1968.
An analysis of traditional polyphonic techniques used by the Yemenite Jews, such as organum, heterophony, canonic imitation, and
their relation to social and religious custom.

_____. "Wedding Dances and Songs of the Jews of Bokhara." Journal of
the International Folk Music Council 2:17-18 1950.
The dances and songs are related to other Jewish communities,
including the Yemenite.

_____. "Women's Songs from the Yemen: Their Tonal Structure and
Form." The Commonwealth of Music, pp. 97-103. Edited by
Gustave Reese and Rose Brandel. In honor of Curt Sachs. New
York: W. W. Norton, 1965.
Originally read as a paper at the 11th Congress of the International
Folk Music Council, Liege, Belgium, 1958.

GESHURI, Me'ir Simeon. "Senunit rišona le-Neginat ha-Mizrach l'Eretz
Yisrael" [The First Swallow of the Music of the East in Palestine].
Die Chazanim Welt (Vienna) 2:23-4 June 1935. In Yiddish.

_____. "The Music of Israel and Its Future." Hallel (Jerusalem) 1:51-3
n3 1930. In Hebrew.

GORALI [Bronzaft], Moshe. Review of Idelsohn's "Lieder der
jemenitischen Juden." From Rešimot (Odessa) 1:3-66 1918.
Kyryath Sefer 8:148-50 n1 January 1930.

GRADENWITZ, Paul. Die Musikgeschichte Israels, von den Anfängen bis zum modernen Staat. Kassel, Basel: Bärenreiter, 1961. 240p See also Musikforschung 17:186-8 n2 1964.

GRADENWITZ, Peter. "Middle East Activities." Hinrichsen's Musical Handbook, vols. 4-5, pp. 340-46. London: Max Hinrichsen, 1947-1948.

_____. The Music of Israel; Its Rise and Growth Through 5000 Years. New York: W. W. Norton, 1949. 334p

GRESSMANN, Hugo. "Musik und Musikinstrumente in alten Testamente." Unpublished dissertation, Giessen, 1903.

HARRIS, Hyman Hirsch. Toledôt ha-Negînah ve-ha-Ḥazzanût be-Yisrael [History of Melody and Cantillation in Israel]. New York: Bazrohn, 1950. 486p In Hebrew.
Hebrew liturgical music, a survey of traditional Hebrew music, biblical cantillation, and the music of the cantors.

HERSKOVITS, Melville J. "Anthropological Basis of Jewish Music." The Jewish Music Forum Bulletin 4:17-19 1943.

_____. "The Work of A. Z. Idelsohn in the Light of Modern Research." The Jewish Music Forum Bulletin 2:6-7 1941.

HERZOG, Avigdor. "Kyryath Tehillim Mizmor 99 Nosah Yehudé Sana'a" [A Way of Reading Psalm 99 by a Jew of Sana'a]. Yesodot Mizrahim v'ma-arravit b'Musikah b'Yisrael [Oriental and Occidental Music in Israel], pp. 27-34. Edited by M. Zorah. Tel Aviv: Israel Music Institute, 1968.

_____., ed. Transcriptions of Yemenite Songs. Renanôt. Tel Aviv: Ha-Makohn ha-Yisraeli l'Musikah Dateet [Israel Institute for Religious Music]. Fasc. 5-6 n1 1959; fasc. 7 n3 1960; fasc. 9 n1 1961; fasc. 10 n1 1962.

_____. "Shirot Teyman" [Yemenite Songs]. Yesodot Mizrahiyyim u'-ma' araviyyim ha-Musikah be-Yisrael [The Oriental and Occidental Musics of Israel], pp. 27-36. Edited by Michal Smoira-Roll. Tel Aviv: Afikim, 1963.

HERZOG, George. "Song, Folk-Song, and Music of Folk-Song." Funk and Wagnall's Dictionary of Folklore, Mythology and Legend, vol. 2, pp. 1032-1050. New York: Funk and Wagnall, 1950.

HOFMAN, Shlomo. "The Destiny of a Yemenite Folk Tune." Journal of the International Folk Music Council 20:25-29 1968. With music. This article questions Tuviah Ovadiah's transcription of the Piyyut (sacred poem) Lannar Velavisomim by the Yemenite poet Sa'adyah, published in the Sabbath Song Collection. Jerusalem: Israel Ministry of Education and Welfare, 1968.

_____. "La Musique Arabe en Israel. Sa Presentation sa Renovation." Journal of the International Folk Music Council 16:258 1964.

_____. "Lannar Velavisomim. Shnai Nosahti Neginah Teyman" [Lanar Velavisomim. Two versions of a Yemenite tune]. Tatzlil 9:150-51 1969.

HOLDE, Artur. "Was unterscheidet orientalische von europäischer Musik?" Der Morgen (Berlin) 11:391-96 November 1935.

HUBBARD, William L., ed. "Music of Primitive (and Oriental) Peoples." American History and Encyclopedia of Music, vol. 3. History of Foreign Music, pp. 1-64. New York: Irving Square, 1910.

IDELSOHN, Abraham Zwi. "Aus den geistigen Leben der echt-orientalischen Juden in Vorderasian, 1, In Yemen; 2, In Persien." Mitteilungen zur jüdische Volkskunde 17:1-9 n1 1915.

_____. "Aus den geistigen Leben der jemenischen (sic) Juden." Ost und West (Illustrierte Monatschrift. Organ der Alliance Israelite Universelle) 14: cols. 213-18 n3 March 1914; 14: cols. 279-86 n4 April 1914. Edited by Leo Winz.

_____. "Der jüdische Volksgesang im Lichte der orientalischen Musik." Ost und West 16: cols. 253-58 n6-7 June-July 1916; 16: cols. 331-43 n8-9 August-September 1916.

_____. "Di folk-melodi fun di orientalische Yidn." Bodn (New York) 2: 43-63 n1 1935. In Yiddish.

_____. "The Distinctive Elements of Jewish Folk Song." Paper delivered at a meeting of the Music Teacher's National Conference. Reproduced in the Music Teacher's National Proceedings. Hartford, Conn., 1924.

_____. Diwân of Hebrew and Arabic Poetry of the Yemenite Jews. With additional notes by Harry Tor Sinai [Torscyner]. Cincinnati: Hebrew Union College, 1930.

_____. Gesänge der jemenitischen Juden. Leipzig: Breitkopf und Härtel, 1914. 158p See also "Širîm Yehudi Teyman." Resimot (Odessa) 1:3-66 1918. In Hebrew.

_____. Hebräisch-orientalischer Melodienschatz, 10 vols. Gesänge der jemenitischen Juden, vol. 1. Leipzig: Breitkopf und Härtel, 1914-1932.
The melodies and texts (the latter in Hebrew, with German transliteration) were transcribed from recordings made in the field (Jerusalem) from 1906, bringing together for the first time in published form, representative and carefully transcribed elements from the Yemenite-Jewish tradition. The series made possible a new era in the study of Jewish music.

_____. Jewish Music in Its Historical Development. New York: Tudor Publishing Co., 1929. Reprint, 1944. xi + 535p

_____. "Die Maqamen der arabischen Musik." Sammelbände der Internationalen Musikgesellschaft 15:1-63 n1 1913-1914.

_____. "Die Maqamen in der hebräischen Poesie der orientalischen Juden." Monatschrift für Geschichte und Wissenschaft des Judentums 57:314-25 n4 April 1913.

_____. "The Mogen Ovos Mode." Hebrew Union College Annual (Cincinnati) 14:1-27 1939.

_____. "Neginah Šemit" [Semitic Melodies]. Ha-Shiloah (Jerusalem) 37: 492-503 n4 1920.

_____. Ozar Neginôt Yisrael, 3 vols.; 5 parts. Jerusalem, Berlin, Vienna: Benjamin Harz, 1922-1928.
This is the Hebrew edition of Idelsohn's Hebräisch-orientalischer Melodienschatz.

_____. "Parallelen zwischen gregorianischen und hebräisch-orientalischen Gesängsweisen," Zeitschrift für Musikwissenschaft 4:515-24 n9-10 June-July 1922.

_____. Phonographierte Gesänge und Aussprachproben des Hebräischen der jemenitischen, persischen und syrischen Juden. Vienna: A. Hölder, 1917. 119p Kaiserliche Akademie der Wissenschaften, Wien. Sitzungsb. Philosophisch-historische Klass. Band 75, Abhandlung 4. Also available in Phonogramm-Archives der Akademie der Wissenschaften in Wien: Katalog 1. Wien: Phonogramm-Archivs-Kommission, 1922. Mitteilung 35. 85p

IDELSOHN, Abraham Zwi. "Reste althebräischen Musik," 1, Jemeniten (Synagogale Weisen der jemenitischen Volkslieder der jemenitischen Juden). Ost und West 12: cols. 571-8 n6 June 1912. 8 sacred music examples, 2 folk song examples. See also Andenken Edmund Birnbaums, vol. 1, pp. 62-9. Sammlung Kantoralwessenschaftlichen Aufsätze. Edited by Aron Friedmann. Berlin: C. Boas, 1922.

_____. "Der Synagogale Gesänge in Lichte der orientalischen Musik." Israelistischen Familienblatt 15:12 n27 July 3, 1913.

KADMAN, Gurit. "Yemenite Dances and Their Influence on the New Israeli Folk Dances." Journal of the International Folk Music Council 4:27-34 1952.

_____. "The Creative Process in Present Day Israeli Dances." Journal of the International Folk Music Council 12:85-6 1960.

KAUFMAN, Ayalah. "Indigenous and Imported Elements in the New Folk Dance in Israel." Journal of the International Folk Music Council 3:55-7 1951.

KAUFMANN, Fritz Mordechai. "Das Folkslied [sic] des Ostjuden." Makkabi. Jüdische Turm- und Sport Zeitung (Berlin) 18:19 n3 March; 13 n4 April; 9 n5 May 1920. See also Kaufmann's Gesammelte Schriften, pp. 246-60. Berlin: E. Laub, 1932.

_____. Die Schönste Lieder der Ostjuden. Berlin: E. Laub, 1920. 152p

KATZ, David. "Culturally Determined Dichotomy in the Musical Practise of Yemenite Jews, with Special Reference to Women's Songs." Unpublished Master's thesis, New York, Jewish Theological Seminary of America, 1969.

KAFAH, Yosef [Yiḥya], ed. Haggadah Teyman. Jerusalem: Yemenite Haggadah, 1958-1959. 176p
Commentaries on the liturgy and the ritual of the Yemenite Haggadah.

KORAH, Amram [Yiḥya]. Sa'arah Teyman [Yemenite Storm]. Edited by Shimon Gri'idi. Jerusalem: Ministry of Culture and Education, 1954. 188p In Hebrew.

_____., ed. Shiri Rabanoh Shalom Shibzi [Rabbinical Songs of Shalom Shibzi]. Jerusalem: Y. Makitohn, 1966. 726p In Hebrew.

_____., ed. Shirim ve-Piyyutot Shalom Shibzi [Songs and Poetry of Shalom Shibzi], vol. 1. Tel Aviv: Yavneh, 1932. Text mainly in Hebrew, with some poems in Arabic set in Hebrew characters.

KUNST, Jaap. Ethnomusicology. The Hague: Martinus Nijhoff, 1959.
303p
Though the body of the text devotes only one line to Yemenite music
as such, the very extensive bibliography carries a fairly substantial
group of bibliographical entries on Yemenite musical subjects.

LACH, Robert. "Orientalisch und vergleichende Musikwissenschaft."
Wiener Zeitschrift für die Kunde des Morgenlandes (Vienna) 29:
463-601 n3-4 1915. [Melodies, pp. 493-94.]

LACHMANN, Robert. "Die Musik der aussereuropäischen Natur- und
Kulturvölker." Handbuch der Musikwissenschaft, vol. 12. Edited
by Ernst Bücken. Wildpark-Potsdam: Akademische Verlags-
gesellschaft Athenaion, 1929. iv + 34p

_____. Jewish Cantillation and Song on the Island of Djerba. Jerusalem:
Hebrew University Archives of Oriental Music, 1940. 115p
The musical practises of the isolated community of Jews on Djerba
(off the coast of Tunisia) are described against the background of
ancient and modern Oriental-Jewish music. Though this work does
not deal with Yemenite music in any specific way, it is included
here because of its import as a pioneering work in the context of
Jewish communities in Islamic environments that have been isolated
for long periods of time from other Jewish communities.

_____. Musik des Orients. Breslau: Ferdinand Hirt, Jedermanns
Bücherei, 1929. 136p

_____. "Musikalische Forschungsausgaben in Vorderen Orient."
Bericht über die Internationalen Sitzung der Geschichte zur
Erforschung der Musik des Orients am 27 April 1930 (Berlin),
pp. 3-21.

_____. "Musiksysteme und Musikaufassung." Zeitschrift für
vergleichende Musikwissenschaft (Berlin) 3:1-23 1935.

_____. "Orientalische Musik auf Schallplatten." Die Musik 24:254-56
n3 1932.
Includes references to recordings of Oriental-Jewish music.

_____. "Preserving Oriental Music." Israel's Messenger (Shanghai) 37:
10-11 December 20, 1940.
About the recordings made for the Archives of Oriental Music at
the Hebrew University in Jerusalem. The same article is printed
in Palestine Review 2:173-74 n1 1934.

LACHMANN, Robert, ed. Zeitschrift für Musikwissenschaft (Organ of the Gesellschaft zur Erforschung der Musik des Orients, later called Gesellschaft für vergleichende Musikwissenschaft). Berlin: Max Hessels Verlag, 1933 (vol. 1); Gesellschaft für vergleichende Musikwissenschaft, 1934 (vol. 2) and 1935 (vol. 3).
All the pertinent articles, as well as the bibliographic references to Oriental-Jewish music from these three volumes have been incorporated into the present bibliography, however, there is much other valuable material in the form of notes, discussions and miscellanea.

LEWIN, B. M. "Iggeret Gaon mi-Babal l'Ertetz Yemen" [Rabbinic Letter from Babylon to the Land of Yemen]. Ginzei-Kedem (Haifa) 3:14-23 1925.

LOEWENSTEIN, Enoch Herbert. "Eine pentatonische Bibelweise in der deutschen Synagoge (um 1518)." Zeitschrift für Musikwissenschaft 12:513-26 n9-10 June-July 1930.

_____. "Ḥokmat ha-Musikah b'mekôrôt Yehudim me-ha-meah 10 v'ad ha-meah 17" [Musical Culture in the Origins of Judaism from the 10th to the 17th Century]. Kyryath Sefer (Jerusalem) 21:187-92 n3 1943-1944. Reprinted in Tatzlil (Jerusalem) 3:158-65 1953.

_____. "Manginot ha-Yehudim be-tave Musikah 'ad shenat 1800" [Notations for Jewish Melodies Before 1800]. Kyryath Sefer 19: 259-63 n4 1942-1943. With 2 examples.
See item for Abraham Yaari for addenda to this article.

MALM, William P. "Jewish Music in the Near East." Music Cultures of the Pacific, the Near East and Asia, pp. 59-61. Englewood Cliffs, New Jersey: Prentice-Hall, 1967.

MAYER, Kathi. "Die Gesänge der orientalischen Juden." Gemeindeblatt der israelistischen Gemeinde (Frankfurt) 5:17 n1-2 September 1926.

MOELLN, Jacob Levi ben Moses [Mahatil]. "Sefer ha-Maharil (Minhagim)" [Wedding Ceremonies with Music and Dance]. Winter und Wunsche. Die jüdische Literatur seit Abschluss des Kanons (Berlin), vol. 2, n49 1897.

MURRAY, Margaret A. "Ancient and Modern Ritual Dances in the Near East." Folklore (London) 66:401-409 December 1955.

NATIONAL JEWISH MUSIC COUNCIL. Bibliography of Articles and Books on Jewish Music. New York: National Jewish Music Council, 1947 and 1955. 53p

_____. Bibliography of Publications and other Resources on Jewish Music. Compiled by Albert Weisser. New York: National Jewish Music Council of the National Jewish Welfare Board, 1969. 117p Revised and enlarged edition of the previous item.

NADEL, Arno. "Jüdische Volkslieder." Der Jude. Songs edited and transcribed by Arno Nadel. Berlin: Benjamin Harz, 1920. 120p

NOY, Meir. "Bibliographia šel Širim Ivrit" [Bibliography of Hebrew Songs]. Tatzlil 1:27-8 1951; 2:101-102 1952. In Hebrew.

OESTERLEY, William Oscar Emil. "The Music of the Hebrews." The Oxford History of Music. Introductory volume, pp. 33-65. Edited by Percy C. Buck. London: Oxford University Press, 1929.

PARISOT, Dom Jean. "A Collection of Oriental Jewish Songs." Journal of the American Oriental Society 24:227-64 part 2 1903.

_____. "Rapport sur une mission scientifique en Turque d'Asie." Nouvelles Archives des Missions Scientifiques et Litteraires, vol. 9, pp. 265-511 1889. Also published in Paris: Ernest Leroux, 1889. 251p
Transcriptions, with words, music and commentary, of 358 songs (mostly religious) of the Maronite, Syrian, Chaldean, Arabic, and Palestinian-Jewish tradition. This work is of interest for evidence of the earliest influences of South-Arabian Jewish music in Palestine, at the period of the beginnings of the Yemenite-Jewish immigration to Palestine.

PARRY, Sir Charles Hubert Hastings. The Evolution of the Art of Music. New York: D. Appelton, 1921. x + 342p Oriental, including Yemenite music, p46.

PINHAS, Heinrich, ed. Fragment eines Gebetbuches aus Yemen; ein Beitrag zur Geschichte der jüdischen und jüdisch-arabischen synagogal-Poesie und zur Kenntnis der arabischen vulgärdialekts in Yemen. Vienna: Commissionsverlag von C. Gerolds Sohn, 1902. 84p See also Jewish Quarterly Review 10:330-33 n2 1903.

PINTHUS, Gerhard Benjamin. "Jüdische Volksmusik in Israel." Completed and edited by Edith Gerson-Kiwi. Musik in Geschichte und Gegenwart, vol. 7, cols. 280-85. Edited by Friedrich Blume. Kassel, Basel: Bärenreiter, 1958.

PORTMAN, M. V. "Oriental Music." Journal, Straits Branch, Royal Asiatic Society 16:422-34 1885.
A proposal for the establishment at Oxford University of 'a complete and exhaustive collection of all musical instruments used throughout the world by the Oriental...'

RATZAHBY, Yehudah. "Ha-Nigun hotzer be-Šir u'-be-Piyyut" [Alien Melodies in Hebrew Music]. Tatzlil 6:13-18 1966. In Hebrew.

_____. "Me-Širat Teyman" [From Yemenite Songs]. Sinai (Haifa) 16: 57-72 n3-4 1952-1953.

_____. "Ravi Šalom Šabazi v'širotoh" [The Songs of Shalom Shabazi]. Sefunot 9:135-66 n1 1964. In Hebrew.

_____. "Piyyôti Teyman: Bibliographia" [Religious Poetry of the Yemenites: A Bibliography]. Kyryath Sefer 22:147-61 n3 1945-1946; 27:378-81 n4 1950.

_____. "Šira ha-iša ha-Yehudim b'Teyman" [Yemenite-Jewish Women's Songs]. Yeda-Am (Journal of the Israel Folklore Society) 5:85-9 n1-2 (21-2) 1958. In Hebrew.
Ratzahby deals with specimens of Jewish women's songs in the Yemen. They are given in the original Arabic vernacular. Aside from any other consideration, women's songs in this isolated community are of especial importance because of their separateness from the men's songs, in both musical archaisms and secular texts. A strong non-Jewish (Arabic) influence is evident in these songs as well, though the Yemenite-Jewish woman seems quite capable of permeating her songs with Jewish musical and textual characteristics. Four songs are given here: two love songs, one hospitality song, and one accouchement song.

_____. "Tsoorah v'lahan b'šira Teyman l'soogiyah" [Toward a Study of the Form and Melody of Yemenite Song]. Tatzlil 8:15-22 1968. In Hebrew.

RAVINA, M. Yemenite Songs. Tel Aviv, 1936. In Hebrew.

RINGER, Alexander L. "Musical Composition in Modern Israel." Musical Quarterly 51:282-97 n1 October 1965.
The article mentions the importance of the influences of Yemenite-Jewish folk music on modern Israeli art music.

ROSOWSKY, Solomon. "The Music of the Pentateuch." Proceedings of the Music Association 60:38-66 1933-1934. Presented in session January 18, 1934.

ROTHMUELLER, Aron Marko. Music of the Jews. New York: Beech-
hurst Press, 1931. 254p

RUBIN, Ruth. "Literature on Jewish Music." Jewish Book Annual 6:
64-70 1947-1948.

SACHS, Curt. Eine Weltgeschichte des Tanzes. Berlin: Reimer und
Vorsohn, 1933; New York: Sensen Arts, 1937. 469p
Deals in part with Arabo-Judaic arts.

_____. Geist und Werden der Musikinstrumente. Hilversum: Fritz A.
M. Knuf, 1965. xi + 282p

_____. History of Musical Instruments. New York: W. W. Norton, 1940.
505p
Contains a section on the Hebraic instrumental environment in
south Arabia in biblical and modern times.

_____. The Rise of Music in the Ancient World. New York: W. W.
Norton, 1943. 324p

_____. Rhythm and Tempo. New York: W. W. Norton, 1953. 391p
Contains a discussion of the Arabic rhythmic modes used by the
Yemenite Jews.

_____. The Wellsprings of Music. Edited and completed by Jaap Kunst.
The Hague: Martinus Nijhoff, 1961; New York: McGraw-Hill, 1965.
228p paperback.
This work mentions the Yemenite-Jewish tradition at several
points, using specific examples of Yemenite-Jewish music.

SANBERG, Mordechai. "Ha-sivoot b'havdalah Tzlili sel Musikah
b'Mizrahit" [The Significance of Tonal Differentiation for the
Music of the East]. Hallel (Jerusalem) 1:58-65 n3 1930. In
Hebrew.

SCHIRMANN, Jefim [Hayyim]. "Verzeichnis des hebräischen Maqamen-
Dichter." Die hebräisch Uebersetzung der Maqamen des Hariri,
pp. 111-32. Frankfurt am Main, 1922.

SCHMIEDER, Wolfgang, ed. Bibliographie des Musikschriftums.
Frankfurt am Main: Hofmeister, 1950-1951, 1958-1959. See
entry under Bibliographie...

SCHNEIDER, Peter. "Bibliographen des Schriftums der hebräischen
Musik." Biblischegeschichtliche Darstellung der hebräischen
Musik, deren Uersprung, Zunahme, ..., pp. 75-90. Bonn, 1834.

SCHOLES, Percy A. "Jewish Music." The Oxford Companion to Music, 3rd ed, revised with an appendix. London, New York: Oxford University Press, 1941. lixi + 1132p [Jewish music, pp. 482-86.]

_____. "Oriental Music." The Oxford Companion to Music, 4th ed, pp. 671-2. London, New York: Oxford University Press, 1942.

SEEGER, Charles. "Oral Tradition in Music." Funk and Wagnall's Standard Dictionary of Folklore, Mythology, and Legend, vol. 2, pp. 1032-1050. New York: Funk and Wagnall, 1950.

SENDREY, Alfred. Bibliography of Jewish Music. New York: Columbia University Press, 1951. xli + 404p
An extensively classified and indexed listing of 10,682 items, including all manner of literature about music, plus editions of actual music and also some recordings. The most recent year of publication noted is for 1944. Other sources take up at approximately the date that Sendrey leaves off. The "Bibliography of Asiatic Musics" in Notes (1948-1949) lists three articles not found in Sendrey. Reviewed by B. Schlochetmann in Kyryath Sefer (Jerusalem) 29:51-2 n1-2 1953.

_____. Music in Ancient Israel. New York: Philosophical Library, 1969. 674p

SHALITA, Israel. Ha-Musikah ha-Yehudit ve-yotzreha [Music of the Jews and Its Creativity]. Tel Aviv: IPC, 1960. 286p

SHILOAH, Amnon. Caracteristiques de l'art Vocal Arabe du Moyen Age. London: Universal Edition, 1964. 235p Reviewed in Musical Opinion 87:374 n1038 March 1964. Mention of Yemenite music.

_____. "Olama šel me-širhat ammamit Teymanit" [A Yemenite Folk Singer]. Tatzlil 9:144-9 1969.

SHMUELI, Herzl. "Oriental Elements in Israeli Song." Journal of the International Folk Music Council 16:29 1964.

SINGER, Jacob. "Music." The Universal Jewish Encyclopedia, vol. 8, pp. 46-54. Edited by Isaac Landmann. New York: Universal Jewish Encyclopedia, 1942.

SMOIRA-ROLL, Michal. Folk Song in Israel. Tel Aviv: Israel Music Institute, 1963. 60p
Commentary on the evolution and historical development of folk song in Israel.

SONKIN, Anabelle B. Jewish Folk Song Resources: An Annotated
Bibliography. New York, 1957. 2p Mimeographed and printed
on one side.

SPARGER, William. "Literature on the Music of the Jews, an Attempt
at a Bibliography." American Hebrew 52:197-9 n1; 229 n2; 265-6
n3 1892.

SPECTOR, Johanna. "A Comparative Study of Scriptural Cantillation and
Accentuation." Unpublished dissertation, Cincinnati, Hebrew
Union College, 1950.

_____. "Anthropological Approach to Jewish Music." Jewish Music
Notes 9:3 October 1954.

_____. "Bridal Songs and Ceremonies from Sana'a, Yemen." Studies in
Biblical and Jewish Folklore, pp. 255-84. Edited by Rafael Patai,
Francis Lee Utley and Dov Noy. Bloomington, Ind.: Indiana
University Press, 1960.

_____. "Further Excusions on the Trail of Oriental Jewish Music." The
Reconstructionist 18:37-43 n2 1955.

_____. "Mekorot l'Musikah ha-Dateet ha-kadoomah b'Yisrael" [Traces
of Ancient Liturgical Music in Israel]. Yeda-Am 4:24-8 n1-2
(19-20) September 1956.
The relation of Yemenite melodies to the second Commonwealth.

_____. "Musical Styles in Near Eastern Jewish Liturgy." Journal of the
Music Academy, Madras (India) 26:122-41 1956.

_____. "Musical Tradition (Yemen)." Encyclopaedia Judaica, vol. 16,
cols. 756-58. Edited by Cecil Roth and Geoffrey Wigodor.
Jerusalem: Keter Publishing Co.; New York: Macmillan, 1971-1972.

_____. "On the Trail of Oriental Music: Among the Yemenites." The
Reconstructionist 18:7-12 n5 1952.

_____. "Yemenite Wedding Songs." The Reconstructionist 24:11-16 n10
1958.

STANFORD, Charles V. and Cecil Forsythe. "The Egyptians, Assyrians,
Babylonians, Hebrews, Arabians, Indians and Chinese." A History
of Music, pp. 15-37. London, New York: Macmillan, 1916.

STEINSCHNEIDER, Moritz. Jewish Literature from the Eighth to the
　　Eighteenth Century... London: Longman, Brown, Green, Longman
　　and Roberts, 1857. ix + 378p, xxii. "The Rhythm and Melody of
　　Hebrew Poetry," pp. 153-6.
　　References to writings on Jewish music in medieval Jewish and
　　Judeo-Arabic literature. Notes on pp. 45, 48, 336-7.

STUTSCHEWSKY, Joachim. Jewish Music. Tel Aviv, 1945.

WALBE, Joel. "Sonographic Analysis of Biblical Readings."
　　Ethnomusicology 11:54-70 n1 1967.

WATERMAN, Richard et al. "Jews, Ancient and Modern." Bibliography
　　of Asiatic Music, Notes 5:354-62 June 1948; 8:549-56 n1-2
　　September 1948.

WELLESZ, Egon. "Probleme der musikalische Orientforschung."
　　Jahrbuch der Musikbibliothek Peters (Leipzig) 24:1-8 1917.

_____. "Vom Wesen der orientalischen Musik." Musik des Anbruch 2:
　　96-9 1920.

WERNER, Eric. Geschichte der jüdischen Volksmusik. Breslau, 1938.

_____. Hebräische Musik; das Musikwerke [Hebrew Music; Anthology of
　　Music], vol. 20. Cologne: Arno Volk Verlag, 1961. 66p

_____. "Jewish Music." Grove's Dictionary of Music and Musicians,
　　vol. 4, 5th ed, pp. 615-36. Edited by Eric Blom. London:
　　Macmillan, 1954.

_____ and Isaiah Sonne. "The Philosophy and Theory of Music in Judeo-
　　Arabic Literatur." Hebrew Union College Annual 16:252-319 1941;
　　16:511-73 1942-1943. Offprint. Cincinnati: Hebrew Union College,
　　1943.

_____. "Prolegomena to a Bibliography of Jewish Music." Historia
　　Judaica 6:175-88 1944.

WIGODOR, Geoffrey. "Music and Dance. Israel, State of (Cultural Life)."
　　Encyclopaedica Judaica, vol. 9, cols. 996-1020. Edited by Cecil
　　Roth and Geoffrey Wigodor. Jerusalem: Keter Publishing Co.;
　　New York: Macmillan, 1971-1972.
　　The influence of Yemenite music on Israeli music, particularly
　　through the popular influences of Braḥa Zfira and Sarah Levi-
　　Tannai.

28

WIORA, Walter. The Four Ages of Music. Translated from the German
   by M. D. Herter Norton. New York: W. W. Norton, 1965. 233p
   Originally published as Die Vier Weltalter der Musik. Stuttgart:
   W. Kohlhammer, 1965. Examples of Yemenite song.

YAARI, Abraham. "Tosafot la-ma'amar hakodem" (Addenda to
   "Manginôt ha-Yehudim be-tave musikah 'ad šenit 1800," by E. H.
   Loewenstein). Kyryath Sefer 19:264-6 n4 1942-1943.

YASSER, Joseph. New Guide Posts for Jewish Music. New York: Jewish
   Academy of Arts and Sciences, 1937. 16p

ADLER, Elkan Nathan. Jews in Many Lands. Philadelphia: Jewish
Publication Society of America, 1905. 259p

ADLER, Marcus Nathan. "The Itinerary of Benjamin of Tudela." Jewish
Quarterly Review 16:453-84 n3 July; 715-33 n4 October 1904; 17:
123-41 n1; 286-306 n2; 514-30 n3; 762-81 n4 1905; 18:84-101 n1;
664-91 n4 1906. See also The Itinerary of Benjamin of Tudela.
London: H. Froude, 1907. English, xvi + 94p; Hebrew, 89p

ALLONI, N. Torat ha Mišklim [The Scansion of Medieval Poetry].
Jerusalem: Hebrew University Press, 1951.

AL-NADDAF, Abraham ben Hayyim. Ḥoveret Šride Teyman [The Book
of the Etronnen Yemenites]. Jerusalem, 1929.

_____. "Le-toldot ha-mesôrēr ha-Tēymani R. Šolom Šabazi" [The Life
of the Yemenite Poet R. Sholem Shabazi]. Mizrach u'Ma'arav
[East and West] 1:227-33 1919.

_____. Sefer Otsar Sefri Teyman [A Treasury of Yemenite Literature].
Jerusalem: Gimi, 1925. 15p

AMERICAN JEWISH YEARBOOK, "Yemen" and "Israel." Philadelphia:
Jewish Publication Society of America, 1937-

ARENDONCK, Cornelius van. De opkomst van het Zaidietische immamat
in Yemen. Leiden: E. J. Brill, 1919. xvi + 348p; Rijkuniversitiet
sichting de Goeje, n5. French translation from the Dutch by Jacques
Ryckmans. Le Debuts de L'immamat Zaidite au Yemen. Leiden:
E. J. Brill, 1960. xvii + 378p

ASSAF, Simḥa. Texts and Studies in Jewish History. Jerusalem:
Hebrew University Press, 1946. 246p

BACHER, Wilhelm. "An Alleged Source of the Jews of Yemen." Jewish Quarterly Review 5:345-7 n1 January 1893.

_____. "Eine angebliche Ergänzung zu Jaḥya Sâlihs Tiklal." Jewish Quarterly Review 15:330-3 n2 April 1903.

_____. Die hebräische und arabische Poesie der Juden Jemens. Strassburg: K. J. Trübner, 1910. 56p   See also Jahrbuch des Landesrabbinerschule in Budapest, pp. 1-54. Budapest: Landes-rabbinerschule, 1910.

_____. "Der Siddur von Jemen." Jewish Quarterly Review 14:740 n4 October 1902.

_____. "Der südarabische Siddur und Jaḥya Sâlihs Commentar zu dem selben." Jewish Quarterly Review 14:581-621 n4 October 1902.

_____. More About the Poetry of the Jews of Yemen; Seven Yemenite Poetical Collections in New York City. Philadelphia: Dropsie College for Hebrew and Cognate Learning, 1912. 55p   Reprinted in the Jewish Quarterly Review (New Series) 2:373-418 n3 1911-1912.

BANETH, D. H. "Geniza Manuscript TS 28.11." J. N. Epstein Jubilee Volume. Edited by Simḥa Assaf. Jerusalem: Hebrew University Press, 1950. 211p

_____. "Michtav me-Teyman me-Shenat 1202" [A Letter from Yemen from 1202]. Tarbiz 20:205-14 1950.

BARER, Shlomo. Al Kanfeh Neshrim. Sipur maktsah "Merved ha-k'simum" [On the Wings of Eagles. The Story of the "Magic Carpet]. Translated from English by R. Alkalay. Tel Aviv: Masada Press, 1954-1955. 194p

_____. The Magic Carpet. New York: Harper and Sons, 1952. xii + 243p

BARON, Salo Wittmayer. A Social and Religious History of the Jews, 8 vols, 2nd ed. "Yemen" 3:69,291; 6:49,78,181,198,204,376; 7:120; 8:64,180. New York: Columbia University Press, 1960. Yemenite romances and literature.

BEN-ZWI, Yitzhak. The Exiled and the Redeemed. Philadelphia: Jewish Publication Society of America, 1957. xiv + 334p   Translated from the Hebrew, Nidhe Yisrael, by Isaac A. Abbady.

_____. "Oriental Jewry and the Upbuilding of Israel." Zion (including the New Judea) 1:23-32 n11-12 1950.

BIEBER, Hugo. "Yemen." The Universal Jewish Encyclopedia, vol. 10, pp. 589-92. Edited by Isaac Landmann. New York: Universal Jewish Encyclopedia, 1942.

BRAUER, Erich. Ethnologie der jemenitischen Juden. Heidelberg: Carl Winters Universitätsbuchhandlung, 1934. xix + 402p Kulturgeschichtliche Bibliothek, n1. Reihe Ethnologisches Bibliothek, n7.

_____. "Die Frau bei den sûdarabischen Juden." Zeitschrift für Sexualwissenschaft und Sexualpolitik 18:152-71 n1 1931.

_____. "Forschungen unter den jemenitischen Juden." Zeitschrift für Ethnologie 63:226-32 1931.

_____. "Yehudi Teyman: Bibliographia" [The Jews of Yemen: A Bibliography]. Kyryath Sefer (Jerusalem) 10:1-35 1933-1934; 11:520-24 n4 1934-1935, with additional notes by A. R. Malachai, pp. 525-29; 12:108 n1 1935-1936, further additions by A. Z. Eshkeli.

BROCKELMANN, Carl. Geschichte der arabischen Literatur. Weimar: E. Felber, 1898-1902; Leipzig: C. F. Amelang, 1901. vi + 265p 3 suppl. volumes published, Leiden, 1937-1942. "Literatur des Osten," vol. 6, 2nd ed. Leiden: E. J. Brill, 1943-1949.

BURCHARDT, Hermann. "Die Juden in Jemen." Ost und West 2: cols. 337-41 n5 August-September 1902.

_____. "Reiseskizzen aus den Jemen." Zeitschrift der Gesellschaft für Erdkunde (Berlin) 12:593-610 1902.

BURY, G. Wyman. The Land of Uz. London: W. Reeves, 1911.

_____. Arabia Infelix, or the Turks in Yemen. London: W. Reeves, 1915. Plate of Yemenite Jew facing p. 30.

BUXTON, Leland. "A Journey to Sana'a." Blackwoods Magazine 179: 597-617 1906.

CARLBACH, Esriel. Exotische Juden: Berichte und Studien. Berlin: Welt Verlag, 1932. 246p

CRUTTENDEN, Charles J. "Narrative of a Journey from Mocha to Sana'a." Journal of the Royal Geographical Society, pp. 267-89. London, 1838.

CORTADA, James N. The Yemen Crisis. Los Angeles, Berkeley: University of California Press, 1965. vii + 31p

FARISSOL, Abraham ben Mordechai. Iggeret Arhôt Olam. Iggeret Teyman [Yemenite Letter]. Prague: Eisenwangerischen Buchdruckerei, 1793. 96p

FARAGO, Laszlo. Arabian Antic. New York: Sheridan House, 1938. 319p

FAROUGHBY, Abbas. Introducing Yemen. New York: Orientalia, 1947. 123p

FEIST, Sigmund. Stammeskunde der Juden; die jüdischen Stämme der Erde in alter und neuer Zeit. Leipzig: J. C. Hinrichs, 1925. 191p

FELDMAN, Joshua. The Yemenite Jews [Die jemenitischen Juden]. London: W. Speaight's Sons; Köln am Rhein: Jüdischer Nationalfund, 1913. 40p

FISCHEL, Walter Joseph. Jews in the Economic and Political Life of Medieval Islam. London: The Royal Asiatic Society, 1937. xi + 139p

_____. "The Region of the Persian Gulf and Its Jewish Settlements in Islamic Times." Alexander Marx Jubilee Volume. New York: Orientalia, 1950.
References to Jewish life in the lower Arabian peninsula.

FORRER, Ludwig. Südarabien nach al-Hamadinis "Beschreibung der arabischen Halbinsul," vol. 28, 3rd in series, Abhandlung für die Kunde des Morgenlandes. Leipzig: Deutsche Morgenländischen Gesellschaft, 1942. 333p

FRAZER, J. G. Folklore in the Old Testament. London: Reeves, 1919.

FRIED, Jacob, ed. Jews in the Modern World, 2 vols. New York: Twayne Publishing House, 1962.

GREIDI, Shimon. "Bibliographia Ivrit Nevḥeret. (Al Yehudi Teyman)" [Selected Hebrew Bibliography: On Yemenite Jews]. Yemenite Literature, pp. 179-87. Edited by Amram ben Yehiyeh. Jerusalem: Hebrew University Press, 1954. In Hebrew and English.

GLASER, Eduard. "Von Hodeida nach Sana'a." Petermanns Mitteilungen 32:1-10 n1; 33-48 n2 1886.

_____. "Meine Reise durch Arḥab und Haschid." Petermanns
Mitteilungen 30:170-83 n6, 204-13 n10 1884.

_____. Sammlung Eduard Glazer, vol. 1. Reise nach Mârib. Edited by
D. H. Müller and N. Rhodokanakis. Vienna, 1913.

_____. "Ueber meine Reisen in Arabien." Mitteilungen der
anthropologischen Gesellschaft in Wien 30:18-27, 77-86 1887.
Originally read as a paper before the Anthropologischen
Gesellschaft, Vienna, October 26, 1886.

GOITEIN, Shlomo Dov Fritz. A Mediterranean Society: the Jewish
Communities of the Arab World as Portrayed in the Documents of
the Cairo Geniza, vol. 1. Berkeley: University of California Press,
1967. Published under the auspices of the Near Eastern Center,
U. C. L. A. 437p

_____. "The Alleged Arabic Origin of Israel and Its Religion." Zion
(Jerusalem) 1:1-18 1937. In Hebrew.

_____. "Evidence on the Muslim Poll Tax." JESHO 6:285 1963.
Concerning the professional and social status of the Yemenite Jew.

_____., ed. "Geniza Document. Bod. ms. Heb. e 11 (cat. 2874)" (from
the Bodlean Library). Zion 17:144-7 1952. In Hebrew.

_____., ed. "Geniza Document. Ts. 12. 179 (Cambridge)." Yerushalayim
2:69-70 n5 1955. In Hebrew.

_____., ed. "Geniza Document. Ts. 13 J. 21 f. 5 1. 17 (Cambridge)."
Alsheikh Memorial Volume, p. 146. Tel Aviv: Israel Publishing
Co. , 1962.

_____. "Temiḥam šel Yehudi Teyman be-Yeshivôt Babal v'-"A"
u'be-Yeshivat ha-Rambam" [The Contribution of the Jews of Yemen
to the Maintenance of the Babylonian and Palestinian Yeshivot and
of Maimonedes School]. Tarbiz (Jerusalem) 31:357-70 n4 July
1962. In Hebrew.

_____. "Ha-yesodôt ha-Ivri b'sfat ha-dibbur šel Yehudi Teyman"
[Hebraic Elements in the Daily Speech of the Yemenite Jews].
Lesônenu 3:356-80 1931. In Hebrew.

_____. Jemenica. Sprichworter und Redensarten aus Zentral-Jemen.
Leipzig: O. Harassowitz, 1934. xxiii + 194p

_____. "Jemenische Geschichten." Zeitschrift für Semitistik 8:162-81
1932; 9:19-34 1934.

GOITEIN, Shlomo Dov Fritz. Jews and Arabs; Their Contacts Through the Ages. New York: Schocken Books, 1964. viii + 247p Bibliography, pp. 225-8.

_____. "Yehudim ve-Yehadut be-Ansāb-al-Ašraf šel Baladhuris" [Jews and Judaism in Baladhuris Ansāb-al-Ašraf]. Zion 1:80 1936. In Hebrew.

_____. Jewish Education in Muslim Countries, Based on Records from the Cairo Geniza. Jerusalem: Hebrew University Press, 1962. In Hebrew.
Important aspects of the Judeo-Moslem symbiosis.

_____. "The Language of the Algades. A Dialect Spoken in Lower Yemen." Le-Museon 73:35-394 1960. In Hebrew.

_____. "Life of Ḥayim Hubbāra od Sana'a, Yemen." (Abridged to H. H.). Davar Literary Supplement (Tel Aviv) n141 Kislev 3, 1931. In Hebrew. See also "Knesset Bet H" [The Synagogue of the Family H.]. Davar Literary Supplement n197 1932.

_____. "The Medieval Profession in the Light of the Cairo Geniza Documents." Hebrew Union College Annual (Cincinnati) 34:184ff 1963.

_____. "The Origins and Historical Significance of the Present Day Arabic Proverb." Islamic Culture (Hyderabad, India), vol. 26 1952.
Concerning Judeo-Arabic as used in Yemenite musico-poetics.

_____. "Portrait of a Yemenite Weaver's Village." Jewish Social Studies (New York) 17:3-26 n1 1955.

_____. "The Social Services of the Jewish Community as Reflected in the Cairo Geniza Records." Jewish Social Studies 26:3-22 n1 January 1964; 67-86 n2 April 1964.

_____. Studies in Islamic History and Civilization. Leiden: E. J. Brill, 1966. ix + 391p

_____. Tales from the Land of Sheba. New York: Jewish Social Studies, 1947; Schocken Books, 1948. 121p

_____. "M'soōt Habšuš" [Travel in Yemen]. Edoth (Jerusalem) 1: 1941. In Hebrew.

_____., ed. Travels in Yemen by Hayim Habšuš; an Account of Joseph Halevey's Journey to Najran, Written by His Guide Hayim Habšuš. Jerusalem: Hebrew University Press, 1941. In Hebrew as M'Soōt Habšuš. Tel Aviv, 1939.

_____. Von den juden Jemens: eine Anthologie gesammelt, übersetzt und herausgegeben von S. D. F. Goitein. Berlin: Schocken Verlag, 1934. 107p

_____. "Warum ich aus Jemen auswanderte." Translated into German from the original Hebrew by Goitein. Jüdische Rundschau (Berlin) 36:239-51 n31 1931. (This paper was published every Thursday and Friday.)

_____. "Zur heutigen Praxis der Leviatische bei orientalischen Juden." Journal of the Palestine Oriental Society 8:3ff 1933.

GOLDMAN, Shlomo. "Zur Geschichte der Juden Jemens." Zeitschrift für die Geschichte der Juden (Tel Aviv) 5:205-208 n4 1968.

GROHMANN, A. Südarabien als Wirtschaftsgebiet. Vienna, 1917.

HAADNI, Mahalal. Ben Aden ve-Teyman [From Aden and Yemen]. Tel Aviv: Am Ovad, 1947. Series Sefriyah "La Dor" [Library "La Dor"].

HAIG, F. T. "A Journey Through Yemen." Proceedings of the Royal Geographical Society (London) 9:479-90 1887.

HALEVY, Joseph. "Briefe an der Herausgeber über seinen Aufenthalt in Aden." Levanon 6:45-7 n1 1872.

_____. "Rapport sur une mission archéologique dans le Yemen." Journal Asiatique 6:5-98 n19 1872. Also published separately in Paris: Imprimerie Nationale, 1872. 295p

_____. "Voyage au Nedjran." Bulletin de la Société de Geographie de Paris 6:5-31, 249-73, 581-606 n6; 6:466-79 n13 1877.

HARRIS, Walter B. A Journey Through the Yemen. London and Edinburgh, 1893.

HARRY, Myriam. "The Yemenite Jews of Siloé." The United States Courier (New York) April 28 1928 p6.

HELFRITZ, Heinrich [Hans]. Das Chicago der Wuste. Berlin, 1932. References to Jewish Life in Sana'a.

HELFRITZ, Heinrich. Im Lande der Königen von Šaba. Wiesbaden: E.
Brockhaus, 1952. 166p

_____. Land ohne Schatten: die letzten Wunder der Wuste. Leipzig: P.
Liszt, 1934. 234p Including music. See also Land Without Shade.
Translated from the German by Kenneth Kirkness. Introduction by
Dagobert von Mikusen. London: Hurst and Blackett, 1935; New
York: National Travel Club, 1936. 286p

HIRSCH, Leo. Neue Wanderungen in Yemen. Braunschweig: Globus,
1898. 74p

HIRSCHBERG, Hayim Ze'ev [Joachim Hirsch]. Betsel ha-Islamim.
Perekim be-Toldôt ha-Yehudim be'Arzôt ha-Mizrahit ha-tiḥon
[In the House of Islam. Historical Aspects of the Jews in the
Countries and Institutions of the East]. Jerusalem: Youth Aliyah,
1953-1954. 70p

_____. Yisrael be'Aravia [Israel in Arabia]. Jerusalem: Youth Aliyah,
1946; Hebrew University Press, 1947. 110p

_____. Shevut Teyman [Yemenite Captivity]. Jerusalem: Hebrew
University Press, 1945. 234p

_____., Hayim J. Cohn and Yehuda Ratzahby. "Yemen." Encyclopaedia
Judaica, vol. 16, cols. 739-56. Edited by Cecil Roth and Geoffrey
Wigodor. Jerusalem: Keter Publishing House; New York: Mac-
millan, 1971-1972.

HUNTER, F. M. An Account of the British Settlement of Aden in Arabia.
London, 1877.

HURWITZ, Maximilan. Israel's Stepchildren? An Appeal on Behalf of the
Institution of the Yemenite Jews of Jerusalem, Palestine. New
York: American Relief Society for the Yemenite Jews of Jerusalem,
Palestine, 1928. 28p

INGRAMS, William Harold. The Yemen; Imams, Rulers and Revolution.
London: J. Murray, 1963. xi + 164p

JACOB, Harold. The Kingdom of the Yemen: Its Place in the Community
of Nations. Problems of Peace and War, vol. 18. Yemenite Jews,
pp. 131-53. London: Grotius Society, 1933.

JACOBS, Joseph. Jewish Contributions to Civilization. Philadelphia:
The Conat Press, 1919. 334p

JARADI Ahmad ibn Muhammad, al. Aus den Jemen; Hermann Burchardts letzte Reise durch Südarabien. Edited by Eugen Mittwoch, with 28 tables after Hermann Burchardt. Festgabe für den vierten deutschen Orientalistentag in Hamburg. Leipzig: Deutsche Morgenländischen Gesellschaft, 1926. 74p

JAWNELI, Š. "B'Teyman" [In Yemen]. Hapoēl Haṣair (Tel Aviv) 5:16-17 1911-1912. In Hebrew.

_____. "Ha-Yehudim b'kerev ha-aravim b'Teyman" [The Jews Under the Arabs in Yemen]. Davar Literary Supplement (Tel Aviv) n1332, 1338, 1362 1930.

_____. Yehudi Teyman [The Jews of Yemen]. Hapoēl Haṣair 4:2-22 1911-1912.

_____. "Matsav ha-Yehudim b'Teyman" [The Position of the Jews of Yemen]. Adama 1:396-407 n4 1920-1921.

_____. "Me-hatsarôt šel mar Š. Jawneli al-debar nesĩato l'Teyman" [Sholom Jawneli's Account of His Journey to Yemen]. Hapoēl Haṣair 5:19-20 1911-1912.

THE JEWISH ENCYCLOPEDIA, 12 vols. "Yemen," vol. 11, pp. 592-4. Edited by Cyrus Adler. New York: Funk and Wagnall, 1901-1906. Vol. 11, 1905.

J. N. EPSTEIN JUBILEE VOLUME. Edited by Simḥa Assaf, et. al. Jerusalem: Hebrew University Press, 1950. In Hebrew.

JUDAH Ben Shalom of Yemen. "Autograph Letter," (facs.). Jewish Quarterly Review 19:facing 162 n1 1907.

"DAS JUEDISCHE FAMILIENLEBEN IN JEMEN." Die Wahrheit (Vienna) 31:5-6 September 8; 6-7 September 15; 9-10 September 22; 7 September 19 1911. Marriage ceremonies with music and dance, September 15. Excerpt from a report of Yomtov Šemah about the situation of the Yemenite Jews.

KAFAH [Kafih] Yosef [Yiḥya]. Halikhot Teyman [Religious Laws of the Jews of Yemen]. Jerusalem: Ben-Zion Institute, 1961. 344p

_____. "Yekorôt Yisrael b'Teymani l'Ravi Hayim Habšus" [Hayim Habšus's 'History of the Jews in Yemen']. Sefunot 2:246-86 1958. In Hebrew.

KAFAH [Kafih] Yosef [Yiḥya]. Melḥemet Adonai Iraki, Hayim ben
Solomon. Amunat...b'ammitit Hakhmat ha-amat. Teshivot šehivro
...ha-Teyman al ha-Sefer Melhemet Adonai [Warrior of the Lord,
Hayim ben Solomon]. Jerusalem: H. Zuckermann, 1938. 540p
In Hebrew.

_____. "Mezukôt Teyman" [Tribulations of Yemen]. Sefunot 5:399-413
1961.

_____. "Sefer 'Dofi ha-Zeman' l'Ravi Sa'id Sa'adi" [The Book of 'Dofi-
Ha-Zeman' (The Chastisements of Time) of Rav Sa'id Sa'id].
Sefunot 1:185-242 1957. In Hebrew.
This article deals with the work by Sa'id ben Solomon Sa'idi written
in 1726, the first chronicle of the Yemenite Jews. The work dealt
with events befalling the Yemenite Jews during the years between
1717-1726, a time of famine, drought, and forced conversions.
Sa'idi uses anecdotes to relate religious and social conditions. Kafah
used manuscripts of the work from various libraries.

KEREN HA-YESOD (Arm of the Jewish Agency dealing with Immigration).
Yetsiyôt Teyman [Yemenite Departure]. Jerusalem: Keren Ha-
Yesod, 195? unpaged pamphlet In Hebrew.
Deals with Yemenite immigration and emigration to and from
Israel.

KYRYATH SEFER. Revaon l'Bibliographia kley mevatoh šel Beth ha-Sefer
ha-ohlami v'ha-Universita [A Quarterly Bibliographical Review, the
Organ of the Jewish National and University Library]. Volumes 1-46.
Jerusalem: Hebrew University Press, 1924- In Hebrew, with
English summaries.

KORAH, Shlomo. Iggeret Bokhim. Jerusalem: Hebrew University Press,
1963. 183p

KOSEMIHAL, Mahut Ragip. "Relations entre le plus Anciennes Civilisa-
tions." Yollaren Sesi (Istanbul) August 1934.
A comparison of musical forms in Sanskrit, Greek, Sumerian,
Assyrian, Hebrew, etc.

LANDSHUT, Siegfried. "Jewish Communities in the Muslim Countries of
the Middle East." Jewish Chronicle (London) 11:1-102 1950.
A survey prepared for the American Jewish Committee of the Anglo-
Jewish Association.

LESLAU, Wolf. "Texts on Yemenite Folklore." Proceedings of the
American Academy for Jewish Research (New York) 14:221-5 1944.

LEVI, Meir. "L'Derekh ohley Teyman b'Yeshuv v'btnaôt ha-avodah.
Bibliographia" [The Integration of the Yemenite Jewish Immigrants
into the Working Force of the Palestinian Jewish Community].
Hapoel Haşair. Bibliographia (Tel Aviv) 1955-1956. 233p

LEVI, Nahum Yehuda. Me-Tsfonit Yehudi Teyman [Of the Jews of
Northern Yemen]. Tel Aviv, 1962. 352p

MAIMONEDES, Moses (1135-1204). Iggeret Teyman [Letter to the
Yemenites]. Edited by David Holub. Vienna: L. Hahan, 1873. 66p;
New York: Hebrew Union of America, 1950; American Friends for
Hebrew Research, 1952. 205p

MACRO, Eric. Bibliography on Yemen and Notes on Mocha. Coral
Gables, Fla.: University of Miami Press, 1960. vii + 63p

_____. Yemen and the Western World Since 1571. New York: Praeger,
1968. xvi + 150p

MALTZAN, Heinrich von. "Sittenschilderungen aus Südarabien."
Globus (Braunschweig) 21:8-10 n1; 26-9 n2; 103-6 n5; 122-4 n6;
138-40 n7 1872.

_____. Reise nach Südarabien. Braunschweig: Globus, 1873.

MANZONI, Renzo. El Yemen. Rome, 1884.

MARCUS, Jacob Rader. The Jew in the Medieval World; a Source Book.
1315-1791. Cincinnati: The Sinai Press, 1938. xxvi + 504p

MARGOLIOUTH, George. "Gleanings from Yemenite Liturgy." Jewish
Quarterly Review (Old Series) 17:690-711 n4 October 1905.

MARGOLOIWTH, David Samuel. The Relations Between Arabs and
Israelites Prior to the Rise of Islam. London: H. Milford for the
British Academy, Oxford University Press, 1924. 86p

MARTIN, Edward Trueblood. I Flew Them Home; A Pilot's Story of the
Yemenite Airlift, Pamphlet n9. New York: Theodore Herzl
Institute, 1958. 63p

MECKLENBERG, Albert. "Einführung in die Probleme der hebräischen
Metrik." Wiener Zeitschrift für die Kunde des Morgenlandes 46:1-
46 1939.

MISHKOWSKY, Noah. Yidn in Afrikah un Azia [Jews in Africa and Asia].
New York: Posy-Shoulson Press, 1936. 160p In Yiddish.
Deals with the Jews in Africa, Yemen and China.

MITTWOCH, Eugen. Aus den Jemen: Hermann Burchardts letzte Reise durch Südarabien. Leipzig: Deutsche Morgenländische Gesellschaft, 1926. 74p See entry under Jaradi Ahmad ibn Muhammed, al.

NEUBAUER, Adolf. "The Literature of the Jews of Yemen." Jewish Quarterly Review (Old Series) 3:604-621 n3 July 1905.

_____. "Postscript to an Article on 'The Literature of the Jews of Yemen.'" Jewish Quarterly Review (Old Series) 4:164 n1 January 1892.

_____. "Zwei Briefe Obadjahs aus Bartenuro." Jahrbuch für Geschichte der Juden 3:222ff 1863.

NIEBUHR, Carsten. Reisebeschreibung nach Arabien und andern umliegenden Ländern, 2 vols. Copenhagen: Nicolaus Möller, 1774 and 1778. Oriental music and dance, 1:175-85; wedding ceremonies, 1:185-6; mourning ceremonies and wailing women, 1:186-7; plates, musical instruments, 1:180; dancers and musicians, 1:184; wedding procession, 1:186.

PATTAI, Raphael. Israel Between East and West; A Study in Human Relations. Philadelphia: Jewish Publications Society, 1953. 348p

PHILLIPS, Wendell. Qataben and Sheba; Exploring the Ancient Kingdoms on the Biblical Spice Routes of Arabia. New York: Harcourt and Brace, 1955. xvi + 362p

PELESKIN, Jacob. "Dehr Galut Teyman und dehr Bundist dehr Meshiah" [The Yemenite Diaspora and the Relationship to the Messiah]. Zukunft (New York) 20:949-57 n9, 1125-35 n11 1915. In Yiddish.

POZNANSKI, Samuel. "Yemenite Rite." Jewish Quarterly Review 17: 1-24, 189 n1; 388 n2 1905.

_____. "Zum Schriften der südarabischen Juden." Jewish Quarterly Review 14:752-7 n4 1902.

QADRI, H. "Jemen; Land und Leute." Unpublished dissertation, Tübingen, 1923.

RATHJENS, Carl. Jewish Domestic Architecture in Sana'a. Introduction by S. D. F. Goitein. Jerusalem: Israel Oriental Society, Hebrew University Press, 1957. 80p

_____ and Heinrich von Wissmann. Landeskundliche Ergebnisse. Berlin: Deutsche Gesellschaft der Kunde des Morgenlandes, 1934. 393p Yemen, pp. 133-6 and Figure 64.

_____. "Sana'a; eine südarabischen Stadtlandschaft." Zeitschrift der Gesellschaft für Erdkunde (Berlin) 30:329-51 1920.

RATZAHBY, Yehudah. Bo'i Teyman. Me-hakrim ve-tadodôt le-tarboot Yehudi Teyman [Come to Yemen. Studies and Documents Concerning the Culture of the Yemenite Jews]. Tel Aviv: Afikim, 1967. 727p Summary in English. Also published in German as Die aus Jemen Kommenden. Tel Aviv: Afikim, 1967.

_____. "Galut Musa" [The Exile of Musa, A Chapter of Yemenite History]. Sefunot (Jerusalem) 5:339-95 1961. In Hebrew with English summary.
This article deals with the expulsion of the Yemenite Jews in 1676-1681, and their redistribution in Yemen. Ratzahby uses poems, colophons, and business documents as source material.

_____. "Marad Al-Qasim" [The Revolt of Al-Qasim]. Zion 20:32-46 n1-2 1955. In Hebrew with English summary.
This work deals with the period of Turkish rule over Yemen from 1546-1905, and in particular the Yemenite revolt from 1627-1629. This was a period of excessive hardship for the Yemenite Jews, who were caught between the factions. Ratzahby deals with records in Arabic and Jewish sources.

_____. "Shnai Agodôt šel Don Isaac Abarbanel be-Teyman" [Two Legends about Don Isaac Abarbanel Told by Yemenite Jews]. Yeda-Am 4:61-5 n1-2 (19020) 1956. In Hebrew.

_____. "Sifrut Yehudi Teyman" [The Literature of the Yemenite Jews]. Kyryath Sefer 28:125-57 n1 (sub-titled "Maimonedesiana"); 255-78 n3; 394-409 n4 1952; 33:111-117 n1 1955; 34:106-116 n1 1959. In Hebrew.

_____. "Taodôt l'Toledôt Yehudi Teyman" [Sources for the History of the Jews of Yemen]. Sefunot 2:287-302 1958. In Hebrew with English summary.
This article aims at a questioning of the idea of the total isolation of the Yemenite Jews from the rest of the Jewish diaspora. Ratzahby points to the correspondence with Babylon, Spain and Egypt. The article covers the visit of the Naggid, R. Jacob Nethanel Fayumi, to whom Maimonedes wrote his "Letter."

_____., ed. Zechariah al-Dahiri's 'Sefer ha-Musar.' Jerusalem: Hebrew University Press, 1965.
The work includes 45 Maqamat speeches in rhymed prose.

REILLY, Sir Bernard Rawdon. Aden and the Yemen. London: Her Majesty's Stationary Office, 1960. 82p

RESSNER, Lawrence. Eternal Stranger; the Plight of the Modern Jew
from Baghdad to Casablanca. Garden City, N. Y.: Doubleday, 1951.
216p

ROBINSON, Nehemiah. The Arab Countries of the Near East and Their
Jewish Communities. New York: Institute of Jewish Affairs, 1951.
83p

_____. "Jews in Moslem Lands (Yemen)." Jews in the Modern World,
vol. 1, pp. 89-90. Edited by Jacob Fried. New York: Twayne
Publishing House, 1963. 318p

ROSSI, Ettore. L'arabo parlato a Sana'a. Rome: Oriental Institute,
1939. vi + 250p

ROTH, Cecil. The Jewish Contribution to Civilization. London: E.
Reeves, 1938. xv + 357p

SAPHIR, Jacob. Ibn Saphir, Even Saphir [Saphir, the Saphire], 2 vols.
Lyck, 1866 and Mainz, 1874.
Description of Saphir's travels from Jerusalem to Egypt, Arabia,
Yemen, Aden, etc.

_____. Iggeret Teyman ha-Shenit [The Second Yemenite Letter]. Vilna,
1873.

_____. "Etsel ha-Nefeš Edeni." Levanon 3:63-73 n4 1865.

SASSOON, David. "Bo'i Teyman"[Come to Yemen]. Hatsofeh 8:307-316
1924.

_____. "Iggeret Paras v'Teyman" [Persian and Yemenite Letter].
Hatsofeh 9:209-31 1926.

_____. "Lekorôt ha-Yehudim b'Teyman" [History of the Yemenite Jews].
Hatsofeh 15:1-26 1931.

_____. "Megillat Teyman" [The Yemenite Megillah; A Fragment of Mori
Yiḥya Salih's History of the Jews of Yemen]. Hatsofeh 7:1-14 1923.

_____. Ohel David [David's Tent]. Catalogue of the Hebrew Manuscripts
in the Sassoon Library, 2 vols. London, 1932.

SCHAPIRA, David. "An Account of His Trip to London." Athenaeum
(London) n2733:346-7 1879.

_____. "Schapiras Reise in Jemen." Globus (Braunschweig) 38:183-6
1880.

SCHMIDT, Dana Adams. Yemen, the Unknown War. London: Bodley
    Head, 1968. 316p

SCHWARTZ, Shlomo Y. Anašim Hadašim be-harim ha-gevohim [New-
    comers to the Mountains and Heights]. Tel Aviv: Kibbutz
    Hamavhad, 1953. 186p In Hebrew.
    Deals with Yemenite literature.

SCOTT, Hugh. "The Yemen in 1937." Royal Central Asian Society
    Journal (London) 27:21-4 1940.

SEMACH, Yomtov. Une Mission de l'Alliance au Yémen. Paris: Alliance
    Israelite Universelle, 1910.

SERJEANT, Robert Bertram. The Portuguese off the South Arabian
    Coast; Hadhramaut Chronicles, with Yemenite and European
    Accounts of Dutch Pirates off Mocha in the 17th Century. Oxford:
    Clarendon Press, 1963. x + 233p

_____., ed. South Arabian Poetry, vol. 1. London: Taylor's Foreign
    Press, 1951. 114p
    Prose and poetry from the Hadhramaut.

SHULIM, Ochser. "Yemen." The Jewish Encyclopedia, vol. 11, pp. 592-
    4. New York: Funk and Wagnall, 1905.

SHUNAMI, Shlomo. Bibliography of Jewish Bibliographies. Jerusalem:
    Magnes Press of the Hebrew University, 1965. xxiv + 992p + xxiii.
    Yemenite bibliographies, pp. 440-41; Music, pp. 193-9. In Hebrew
    with some English translation, though the use of English translation
    of entries is not used in every case.

SLOAN, George Z. B. "The Kingdom of Yemen." The Sentinel, vol. 15,
    October 10, 1939.
    A weekly Jewish newspaper published in Chicago.

SMITH, William Robertson. Kinship and Marriage in Early Arabia.
    Cambridge: Cambridge University Press, 1885. xiv + 322p
    Revised edition with additional notes by W. R. Smith and Ignaz
    Golziher and edited by Stanley A. Cook. London: R. and C. Black,
    1903. xxii + 324p

STARK, Freya. East Is West. London: John Murray, 1945. xxii + 218p
    Jews in Yemen at the start of World War II. Plate of Yemenite
    Jews.

_____. The Southern Gates of Arabia; a Journey in the Hadhramaut.
    London: J. Murray, 1936. xii + 327p

STARK, Freya. Seen in the Hadhramaut. London: J. Murray, 1938.
xxiii + 199p

STEINSCHNEIDER, Moritz. "Arabic Literature of the Jews." Jewish
Quarterly Review 13:95-110 n1 1901.

_____. Die arabische Literatur der Juden: ein Beitrag zur Literatur-
geschichte der Araber, grossentheils aus handschriftlichen Quellen.
Frankfurt am Main: J. Kaufmann, 1902. liv + 348p
Reviewed by H. Hirschfield in the Jewish Quarterly Review 16:408-
413 n3 1904.

TABIB, Abraham. Golat Teyman [The Yemenite Exile]. Tel Aviv:
Omanuth, 1931. 85p

_____. Šayvih Teyman [Return to Yemen]. Tel Aviv: Omanuth, 1932.
95p

TAILLARDAT, F. "L'Arabie du Sud. Hadramaout et Yémen." Asie
Française (Paris) 37:210-14, 237-44 n2 1937.

TRITTON, A. S. The Rise of the Imams of Sana'a. London: H. Milford,
1925. 141p

VAYSSIERE, A. and Thomas Arnaud. "Les Akhdam de l'Yémen leur
origine probable, leurs moeurs." Journal Asiatique (Paris) 4:376-
87 n15 1850.

VERED, Yael. Ha-Fikal ve-Malkhamah be-Teyman [Coup and War in
Yemen]. Tel Aviv: Am Ovad, 1967. 251p In Hebrew.

VON DER JUEDEN JEMENS. Berlin-Wilmersdorf: Orient Verlag, 1913.
30p Printed under the auspices of Hilfskomittee für die
jemenitischen Juden, Berlin.

WEBERS, Otto. "Eduard Glasers Forschungsreisen in Südarabien."
Der Alte Orient (Leipzig) 18:1-34 n4 1907.

WEISSENBERG, Maurice. "Die jemenitische Juden." Zeitschrift für
Ethnologie; Organ für deutschen Gesellschaft für Völkerkunde 41:
314-37 1908.

WENER, Manfred W. Modern Yemen, 1918-1966. Baltimore: John
Hopkins Press, 1967. 257p

WOLFF, Reverend Joseph. Journal of the Reverend Joseph Wolff, in a Series of Letters to Sir Thomas Baring, Containing an Account of His Missionary Labours from the Years 1835 to 1838. London, 1839. 523p The Jews of Yemen, pp. 391-402.

WREDE, Adolf von. Adolf von Wredes Reise in Hadhramaut. Edited by Heinrich von Maltzan. Braunschweig: Globus, 1870.

YEMENI, Yehoshua. Roshe-perakim be-mavo le-Tanach. Tiberias: Kanrat, 1942. 79p

YISHAYAHU, Israel, ed. Me-Teyman l'Zion [From Yemen to Zion]. Tel Aviv: Masada, 1938. 295p In Hebrew.

ZADOC, Moshe. Yehudi Teyman. Tolodôteiḥem v'orḥot hayyeiḥem [The History of the Jews of Yemen]. Tel Aviv: Am Oved, 1967. 270p

Folk Dances. Folk (FE), vol. 4
   The Middle East, including Yemen.

Folk Music of the Mediterranean. Folk (FE) 4501/a-d
   Selections and notes by Henry Cowell.
   Includes areas of Algeria, Sardinia, Albania, Syria, France, Egypt,
   Morocco, Italy, Tunis, Greece, Turkey, Spain, Serbia, Libya and
   Palestine.

Folk Music of Palestine. Ethnic Folkways. Folk (FE) 4408
   Recorded by the Department of Folk Music, Anthropological Institute
   of Israel. Introduction by Raphael Pattai, notes and transcriptions
   by Mieczyslaw Kolinski.
   Includes areas of Bokhara, Palestine, Yemen, Persia; instruments:
   doyra, tar, durbukki, qanun.

Hebrew Folk Songs. Ethnic Folkways. Folk (FE) 6928

HERZOG, George. A collection made in 1939-1941 on discs.
   Recorded in New York City by native cantors representing the
   Babylonian and Yemenite traditions. There are 189 discs, mostly
   of sacred character, of the Babylonian tradition, and 68 discs,
   also mostly of sacred character, of the Yemenite tradition.

IDELSOHN, Abraham Zwi. A collection made in 1913-1916 on cylinders.
   Phonogram-Archiv der Kaiserliche Akademie der Wissenschaft,
   Vienna, 1922. Edited by Dr. Sigmund Exener for the Phonogramm-
   Archivs-Kommission. Katalog 1,200 cylinders, including 25
   recordings of Yemenite secular and sacred song as well as language.
   Also available in Phonogram-Archiv der Völkerkundliche Museum,
   Berlin. Both collections existed only until 1945. See Idelsohn's
   listing.

Israel. Ethnic Folkways. P. 408 (4408)
>   Yemenite bible cantillation; Song of Moses (Exodus); Hebrew liturgy.
>   Cantor Zion Nahar, 26 years old, born in Sana'a.
>   Recorded in Jerusalem on June 16, 1947, while Nahar was in the
>   army.
>
>   Yemenite Ceremonial Wedding Song, sung with male chorus along
>   with "magic cries" by women, in Hebrew and accompanied by
>   derbuka, drums, bones and metal gong.
>   Recorded on September 15, 1947, by Yehiel Adaki, ca. 50 years
>   old, who was born in Sana'a and is resident of Tel Aviv.

LACHMANN, Robert. A large collection made in 1920-1927 on discs.
>   Located at the Jerusalem Sound Archiv for Oriental Music at the
>   Hebrew University.

Music of South Arabia. Ethnic Folkways. Folk (FE) 4421
>   Music of the Bedouin and Yemenite Jews, recorded with notes by
>   Wolf Leslau at the Hashed Camp, Aden, 1950.

National Sound Archives (in the Jewish National and University Library,
Hebrew University in Jerusalem)
>   Includes recordings made by Idelsohn, Lachmann and Spector. Up
>   to 1971 there were more than 15,000 items stored. The Archive
>   has existed since 1964.

Oriental Songs. Greater 74

Songs of Yemen and Israel. Vanguard 9125

Yemenite Passover: The Hagadah. Ethnic Folkways. Folk (FN) 8921
>   Recorded by Sam Eskin. Notes by Theodor Gastner.

Titles in the
Detroit Studies in Music Bibliography
Series:

General Editor:

Bruno Nettl
University of Illinois at Urbana-Champaign

note: all dsmb's are paperbound except where indicated

1
Reference Materials in Ethnomusicology, *by Bruno Nettl*
Rev ed 1967   54p   ISBN 911772-21-9 $2.00

2
Sir Arthur Sullivan: An Index to the Texts of His Vocal Works, *compiled by Sirvart Poladian*
1961   91p   ISBN 911772-22-7 $2.75

3
An Index to Beethoven's Conversation Books, *by Donald W. MacArdle*
1962   46p   ISBN 911772-23-5 $2.00

4
General Bibliography for Music Research, *by Keith E. Mixter*
1962   38p   ISBN 911772-24-3 $2.00

5
A Handbook of American Operatic Premieres, 1731-1962, *by Julius Mattfeld*
1963   142p   ISBN 911772-25-1 $3.00

6
Medieval and Renaissance Music on Long-Playing Records, *by James Coover and Richard Colvig*
1964   122p   ISBN 911772-26-X $3.00

7
Rhode Island Music and Musicians, 1733-1850, *by Joyce Ellen Mangler*
1965   90p   ISBN 911772-27-8 $2.75

8

Jean Sibelius: An International Bibliography on the Occasion of the
Centennial Celebrations, 1965, *by Fred Blum*
1965   114p   ISBN 911772-28-6 $3.50

9

Bibliography of Theses and Dissertations in Sacred Music, *by Kenneth R. Hartley*
1967   127p   ISBN 911772-29-4 $3.00

10

Checklist of Vocal Chamber Works by Benedetto Marcello, *by Caroline S. Fruchtman*
1967   37p   ISBN 911772-30-8 $2.00

11

An Annotated Bibliography of Woodwind Instruction Books, 1600-1830, *by
Thomas E. Warner*
1967   138p   ISBN 911772-31-6 $3.00

12

Works for Solo Voice of Johann Adolf Hasse, 1699-1783, *by Sven Hostrup Hansell*
1968   110p   ISBN 911772-32-4 $3.00

13

A Selected Discography of Solo Song, *by Dorothy Stahl*
1968   90p   ISBN 911772-33-2 $2.50
Supplement, 1968-1969, *by Dorothy Stahl*
1970   95p   ISBN 911772-34-0 $2.50

14

Music Publishing in Chicago before 1871: The Firm of Root & Cady, 1858-1871,
by Dena J. Epstein
1969   243p   ISBN 911772-36-7 $6.00

15

An Introduction to Certain Mexican Musical Archives, *by Lincoln Spiess and
Thomas Stanford*
1969   85+99p   ISBN 911772-37-5 $3.50

16

A Checklist of American Music Periodicals, 1850-1900, *by William J. Weichlein*
1970   103p   ISBN 911772-38-3 $3.00

17

A Checklist of Twentieth-Century Choral Music for Male Voices, *by Kenneth
Roberts*
1970   32p   ISBN 911772-39-1 $2.00

18

Published Music for the Viola da Gamba and Other Viols, *by Robin de Smet*
1971   105p   ISBN 911772-40-5 $3.00

19

The Works of Christoph Nichelmann: A Thematic Index, *by Douglas A. Lee*
1971   100p   ISBN 911772-41-3 $3.50

20

The Reed Trio: An Annotated Bibliography of Original Published Works,
by James E. Gillespie, Jr.
1971   84p   ISBN 911772-42-1 $4.75

21

An Index to the Vocal Works of Thomas Augustine Arne and Michael Arne,
by John A. Parkinson
1972   82p   ISBN 911772-45-6 $3.50

22

Bibliotheca Bolduaniana: A Renaissance Music Bibliography, *by D. W. Krummel*
1972   191p   ISBN 911772-46-4 $6.50   clothbound $8.00

23

Music Publishing in the Middle Western States before the Civil War, *by Ernst C. Krohn*
1972   44p   ISBN 911772-47-2 $4.00

24

A Selected Discography of Solo Song: A Cumulation through 1971, *by Dorothy Stahl*
1972   137p   ISBN 911772-35-9 $5.00   clothbound $6.50

25

Violin and Violoncello in Duo without Accompaniment, *by Oscar R. Iotti, based on the work of Alexander Feinland*
1973   73p   ISBN 911772-48-0 $4.25   clothbound $5.75

26

Medieval and Renaissance Music on Long-Playing Records: Supplement,
1962-1971, *by James Coover and Richard Colvig*
1973   258p   ISBN 911772-44-8 $7.00   clothbound $8.50

PUBLICATIONS IN PROGRESS

Solos for Unaccompanied Clarinet: An Annotated Bibliography, *by James E. Gillespie*

Claude Debussy: A Bibliography, *by Claude Abravanel*

Titles in the
Detroit Monographs in Musicology
Series:

Editorial Committee:

Albert Cohen
State University of New York at Buffalo

Bruno Nettl
University of Illinois at Urbana-Champaign

Albert Seay
Colorado College

Howard Smither
University of North Carolina

1
The Beginnings of Musical Nationalism in Brazil, *by Gerard Behague*
1971   43p   ISBN 911772-50-2 $5.00

2
Daramad of Chahargah: A Study in the Performance Practice of Persian Music,
by Bruno Nettl with Bela Foltin, Jr.
1972   84p   ISBN 911772-51-0 $6.00